The Tragedy of Macbeth

Illustrated by: Suman S. Roy
Compiled and Edited by: Manpreet K. Aden

Contents

1. The Tragedy of Macbeth at a Glance 3

2. Who's Who in the Play 4

3. The Tragedy of Macbeth 6

4. Post-reading Activities 42

5. About the Author 43

The Tragedy of Macbeth at a Glance

Macbeth is certainly Shakespeare's most powerful and emotionally intense play. The play is fast paced where one thing leads to another until the play ends. It is Shakespeare's shortest and also the bloodiest tragedy. A *tragedy* is a play that is based on human suffering. It is a literary work in which the main character is destined to get ruined and hence he suffers extreme sorrow.

Macbeth was written around 1606. The play is unique in many ways most notably so because it dealt with material that was relevant to England's political situation.

Who's Who in the Play

Macbeth

Macbeth is a Scottish general and the thane of Glamis. He is ambitious, fearful, and easily persuaded.

Lady Macbeth

She is the wife of Macbeth. She is an extremely ambitious woman, is ruthless and wants power.

Banquo

He is a noble general in King Duncan's army. Unlike Macbeth, he is sceptical about the witches' prophecy. He is not ambitious.

King Duncan

He is the righteous and benevolent ruler of Scotland. His murder symbolizes the destruction of law and order in Scotland.

Macduff

He is a Scottish nobleman who had opposed Macbeth from the beginning. He joins Malcolm, King Duncan's son, in his war against Macbeth.

The Witches

These are three hags who plot mischief against Macbeth by using charms and by brewing potions. Their true identity remains unclear in the play.

The Tragedy of Macbeth

During the time when Duncan the Meek was the reigning King of Scotland there lived a great thane, or lord, called Macbeth. Macbeth was also a relative of the king. He was greatly respected at the court for his valour and conduct during the wars. It was the same valour that he had shown in defeating a rebel army that had been assisted by the troops of Norway. The rebels had eventually lost the war owing terrible loses because of Macbeth's courage.

The two Scottish generals, Macbeth and Banquo, were returning victorious from this war against the Norwegians. Their spirits were high as they

Glossary
Reigning it is the duration of time when a king rules over a region
Valour great courage, bravery especially during war

made their way over a vast wasteland. There were thunder clouds in the sky and the wind had picked up speed. The weather was getting worse. 'I have never seen such a day which was good and bad

Glossary
Wasteland a piece of land that can no longer be used to grow crops

at the same time,' said Macbeth referring to the war they had won and the bad weather. Suddenly, they saw three figures standing in the distance. It seemed as if the figures were waiting for Macbeth and Banquo.

The two generals made their way towards the figures whom they saw were crazily dressed and had withered skin. 'Who are you?' asked Macbeth, 'you appear like women yet your beards fill me with confusion. Where have you three come from? Do you even live on this earth?' Macbeth fell silent saying this. Then, a figure among the three broke the silence. The woman saluted Macbeth and said, 'All hail! Thane of Glamis!' Macbeth wasn't surprised to hear this. Then the second woman saluted Macbeth and said, 'All hail Macbeth! Thane of Cawder!' Then the third saluted Macbeth with these words, 'All hail Macbeth, the future king!' Macbeth was stunned into silence.

Macbeth knew that as long as the king's son lived he would not be king, so this prophetic greeting amazed him. While Macbeth was thus startled, the three women had turned to Banquo. The

Glossary
Withered something which has become dry or has died; something old and weak
Prophetic telling or showing what will happen in the future

first said, 'You are lesser than Macbeth but also greater!' The second woman then said, 'You are not as happy as Macbeth, but much greater!' Then, the third stepped forward and said, 'Though you won't be king but your descendants will be.' Then, together the three witches said, 'All hail Macbeth and Banquo!' The next moment, the three women turned into air and vanished! Macbeth and Banquo realised that the three women were the weird sisters or witches.

As they stood there thinking about the strangeness of the meeting which had just taken place, they saw the king's messengers coming towards them. 'What brought you here, my friend?' asked Macbeth.

'Hail to the thane of Cawder!' said the messengers.

'Why do you address me so? The thane of Cawder is alive and I am not he,' said Macbeth.

'Yes, the Thane of Cawder is alive but he has been sentenced to death for his treason. You, my lord, have been bestowed with the title of Thane of Cawder,' explained the messenger.

Glossary
Vanished to go out of sight suddenly; disappear
Treason to do something that can put your country or state in danger; betray trust

Macbeth and Banquo remained silent for some time for the witch's prophecy had come true. It was at this moment that the hope that he would be the King of Scotland took root in Macbeth's heart and mind. Macbeth was brave and loyal but he was also ambitious and wanted the best possible position that he could aspire to for himself. He had always wanted to be the King of Scotland.

'It can be a mere coincidence,' said Banquo reading Macbeth's face. 'Often the agents of evil partly tell us the truth

Glossary
Ambitious someone who wants to be rich, powerful and successful

to lead us to our destruction.' But Macbeth was already too far gone in his thoughts. He now aspired to be the King of Scotland.

Macbeth, Banquo and the king's messengers, after a while, went to meet King Duncan who greatly praised Macbeth and Banquo. He also pronounced that he has decided to make his son Malcolm, the heir apparent. 'Now, Macbeth let us move to your castle at Inverness and let me have a taste of your hospitality,' said King Duncan turning to Macbeth. 'I shall go ahead and tell my wife to make adequate preparations,' said Macbeth.

Soon, Macbeth reached the Inverness Castle. He went to his wife, Lady Macbeth and told her about the strange prediction made by the weird sisters. He also told her about the partial fulfilment of the prophecy. The demeanour of Lady Macbeth seemed to change as she heard the events told by her husband. Now, she was an ambitious and ruthless woman who would stop at nothing to get what she wanted. When she had heard everything, she said, 'If it is said that you, my dearest, must become king then you must be a king. You are

Glossary
Apparent something which is easy to see or understand
Partial part of something; incomplete
Demeanour it is the way that someone looks or behaves
Ruthless someone who is hard and cruel; pitiless

too kind to grab the opportunity that has come your way. You want to be powerful but you lack the meanness required to become powerful. But I will persuade you to do what it needs to have the crown on your head.'

They were still talking when a messenger came out of breathe and announced that King Duncan had just entered the castle accompanied by his sons Malcolm and Donalbain and a number of Lords and attendants. Lady Macbeth could hardly believe that fate was on her side as evil thoughts took root in her head.

'My lord, let us go and receive the king,' said Lady Macbeth. 'But be careful, my lord, for your expressions betray the thoughts in your heart. Keep smiling like a flower but be a snake that hides under the flower.'

'We will talk about this later,' said Macbeth. Together, they went to receive the king. Meanwhile, Macbeth had understood the meaning of Lady Macbeth's words but he remained reluctant to commit a murder. He knew what a

Glossary
Reluctant the hesitation before one does something

scandal it would become if the king was murdered in his castle on the day he had been honoured by the king. He also admitted that the only thing that will spur him to commit the murder would be his ambition which he knew would lead him to his destruction.

Later, when the king had had his dinner, he once again asked for Macbeth who had not been with him since his arrival in the Inverness Castle. Lady Macbeth went to fetch her husband. When she met him, Macbeth asked, 'Has he asked for me?'

'He has been asking for you all evening,' said Lady Macbeth. 'What? Have you got cold feet now that you are so close to fulfil your ambition to be the king?'

'This is wrong! The king had just honoured me with a title and I should not betray him in this manner,' argued Macbeth. 'Besides, it is my duty as the host to protect the king from his enemies and not kill him myself. It is unethical! What if I fail?'

'What if we fail? But you would not fail. Gather

Glossary
Betray to break someone's trust in you by helping their enemy
Unethical unprincipled; not acceptable on moral grounds

up your courage,' encouraged Lady Macbeth so that Macbeth could murder King Duncan to be king himself. 'The king is sleeping already as the long journey he undertook today had tired him. Only two grooms are in his chamber. Leave it to me to get them drunk. When they are drunk, you and I can do what we want. Duncan would be completely unguarded. Afterwards, we can put the blame on the grooms.'

Thus, the plot to kill King Duncan had been settled where Lady Macbeth was the force that urged Macbeth to commit the murder. Macbeth was convinced that this act was necessary if they wanted power and position. Now was the middle of the night, when over half the world had fallen asleep. It is the time when wicked dreams abuse men's minds and none but the wolf and the murderer are awake to commit murder. This was the time when Lady Macbeth woke up to fulfil the plot of murdering the king. She knew that the king must be murdered tonight as her husband was in her power. Even a slight delay was enough to change her husband's mind. She had won his

Glossary
Abuse to do something wrong or to mistreat someone

consent to commit the murder but she doubted his resolution. She feared that her husband's natural kindness was enough to defeat their purpose. So, holding a dagger in her own hands, she approached the king's bed. Her intoxicated wine had worked for the grooms were lost in the world of dreams and were careless of their charge. Lady Macbeth watched King Duncan as he lay fast asleep in the bed, fatigued by his journey. As she watched him earnestly, she felt that the king's face resembled her own father's, and she did not have the courage to proceed and kill the king.

So, she went out of the king's chamber and went to seek her husband. Meanwhile, Macbeth was walking towards the king's chamber with a dagger in his hand. He softly opened the door to the king's chamber and saw the king fast asleep. Just as he took a step in the darkness, he saw another dagger in the air. The dagger's handle was turned towards him and on its blade and at its point were drops of blood.

'Is that a dagger that I see in front of me,' said Macbeth. 'Come, let me hold you.' But just as

Glossary
Consent to permit someone to do something
Intoxicated so excited that one is unable to think clearly
Fatigued someone who is tried both physically as well as mentally

he tried to grab the dagger, his hands touched nothing but air. 'An apparition! I don't have you but I can still see you,' said Macbeth. 'You are leading me towards the place where I was already going and I was planning to use a weapon just like you.'

Then, as he saw his goal in sight, Macbeth was filled with confidence and he stepped towards the king's bed. He heard the two grooms as they laughed and murmured words while intoxicated with sleep. Suddenly, the servants woke for one among them had an unpleasant dream. Quickly one among them said his prayers and finished them saying, 'God bless us,' and the other said, 'Amen'. Soon after saying their prayers, the two servants fell asleep again. Macbeth, who had stood listening to them, had tried to say 'Amen' but, though he needed a blessing the most, the word remained stuck in his throat and he could not say it.

Soon, Macbeth returned to his wife, Lady Macbeth. Though at first, she suspected that her husband might have lost courage at the last moment. But then she saw the bloody dagger

Glossary
Apparition a figure that appears suddenly; resembling a ghost
Murmured speaking in a low voice that is difficult to hear

in her husband's hand. 'The deed is done,' said Macbeth.

'My lord, why did you carry these daggers out of the room? Please go and wash your hands that are stained by blood.' Then, Lady Macbeth quickly took the dagger from Macbeth's hand. 'I will go back and smear the sleeping grooms with the blood. We must make it appear that the grooms are guilty.' Macbeth by this time had already started getting pricked by his conscience for killing King Duncan.

In the morning, Macduff discovered the king's murder when he came to wake up the king. 'Horror! Horror! The king has been murdered!' Macduff came crying as Macbeth, Lennox and Banquo stood talking. Unable to believe their ears, Macbeth and Lennox rushed to the king's chamber. They returned minutes later and saw that the king's sons Malcolm and Donalbain too had woken up hearing the cry rising in all directions.

'I saw the king's grooms covered with blood and their daggers sparkling with fresh blood,' lamented

Glossary
Smear to spread a substance over something or someone in a careless manner
Lamented to express sorrow over the loss of something or someone; grief, weeping

Macbeth. 'I could not contain my rage and killed the grooms for taking our beloved king away from us.'

'Why did you do such a reckless deed?' said Banquo.

But the damage had already been done. Meanwhile Lady Macbeth too had heard the cries and pretended to be so grief-stricken that she fainted. Then, amid this chaos the king's sons were suspected of murdering their father. Meanwhile, Duncan's two sons also felt that someone close to them had accomplished this horrible deed. They decided that for now it was wiser to flee from Scotland. Malcolm, the eldest, thus sought refuge in the English court while the younger, Donalbain, escaped to Ireland.

Meanwhile, it was planned to look for the murderer of King Duncan. Now as the king's sons, who were heirs to the throne had vacated it; Macbeth was next in line to be crowned king as he was a close relative of the king. Thus the prediction of the weird sisters that Macbeth would become the King of Scotland had literally been accomplished!

Though now the ambition of Macbeth and his queen had been accomplished, yet they were not satisfied.

Glossary
Reckless to do something without caring about the dangers involved; careless
Literally it means to emphasize the truth of something which can be surprising

The cause of their restlessness was the prophecy of the weird sisters where the sisters had predicted that though Macbeth would be king but not his children. Also, the children of Banquo would be kings after Macbeth. The thought that they had

smeared their hands with blood, and done so great a crime, only to see the sons of Banquo sit upon the throne was an idea unbearable to them. It was in this vicious atmosphere that Macbeth thought of an evil plan to make his ends meet. He plotted to kill Banquo and his son, so that the predictions of the weird sisters would not be fulfilled and his own descendants would rein as kings!

Macbeth then hired two murderers who were to kill Banquo and his son Fleance. Then, the new king and queen of Scotland organised a great supper. To this supper, they invited all the chief thanes and most importantly, they invited Banquo and his son Fleance. Later that night, while the banquet had started, Banquo and his son were on their way to the palace. But the two murderers were waiting for them to attack them and kill them. When they crossed the murderers, the murderers attacked them. During the ambush that followed, Banquo was stabbed by the murderers but Fleance managed to escape during the scuffle. Another of Macbeth's evil plans had been accomplished.

Glossary
Vicious aggressive, dangerous and violent atmosphere or person
Supper a light meal eaten at the end of the day
Ambush to hide and then attack someone; a surprise attack

At supper, Lady Macbeth, now the queen, played the role of the hostess with the gracefulness and attention which was liked by all the assembled guests.

'I am honoured to have such a noble company under my roof,' said Macbeth greeting his guests. 'I welcome you all. Only if my good friend Banquo were also present. I just hope that he is late due to rudeness and not because some mishap had taken place. Please be seated and I raise a toast to you all.'

Saying this, Macbeth turned towards his chair to occupy. Meanwhile, Banquo's ghost had

Glossary
Mishap an accident which may not have serious results

entered the room and had occupied the chair which Macbeth was about to sit on. Though Macbeth was a bold man, and one that could have faced the devil without any fear in his heart, now turned pale and

stood unmanned staring at the ghost sitting on his chair.

'Is something wrong, Your Majesty?' asked the nobles.

Lady Macbeth understood that perhaps her husband was again gripped by his fear of being discovered, so she said, 'Please, do not leave. It is merely a fit from which My Lord has been suffering since childhood. Pay no attention to him and resume your supper.'

'What I see will even scare the devil,' whispered Macbeth, frightened.

'Ah, nonsense! It is merely one of your hallucinations like the one you saw involving the dagger in the air when you were about to kill Duncan,' Lady Macbeth reproached her husband in a whisper.

'Please, look over there. What do you see?' said Macbeth frightened. But just as Macbeth said this, the ghost disappeared. But as Macbeth continued to talk of ghosts, Lady Macbeth hastily dismissed the feast. Meanwhile, Macbeth was tormented

Glossary
Unmanned something that does not need a person to control it
Hastily something done or said very quickly
Tormented a great mental or physical suffering; misery

by such dreadful hallucinations that he found no peace. At last, Macbeth decided to once more seek out the weird sisters. 'They will tell me more for I want to know from them the worst that is going to happen. My safety is the most important thing at this moment. I have gone too far in this river of blood. I cannot go back to being good.'

Soon, Macbeth went to visit the three witches. He found them in a cave upon the heath, where they, who already knew that Macbeth would come, were busy making charms to conjure up infernal spirits. 'We know why you are here,' said the witches as they continued to stir the various ingredients in their cauldron. 'Keep quiet and listen.' By these charms, they bound three spirits to answer Macbeth's questions.

The first spirit that arose looked like an armed head. It said, 'Beware Macbeth of Macduff, the Thane of Fife.' Saying this, the first spirit vanished. The second spirit that appeared like a bloody child arose next. It said, 'Macbeth, have no fear. Laugh at the power of other men, for nobody born from a woman shall harm you.' Macbeth is happy to

Glossary
Conjure to make something appear; magic
Infernal something or someone connected with hell

hear this. Then, a third spirit arose in the form of a child crowned, with a tree in his hand. It said, 'Macbeth, do not be troubled by conspiracies and those who hate you, for you shall never be

harmed until Birnam Wood comes to fight you on Dunsinane Hill.'

'Ah! That appeases my troubled soul,' said Macbeth. 'Who can ask the forest trees to uproot themselves? I shall reign as king during my whole life. Yet my heart wants to know one thing. Please tell me, whether Banquo's descendants shall be kings?'

The next moment, the cauldron sank into the ground, and amidst music eight kings marched in front of Macbeth. The last among them carried a mirror in which appeared many more men followed by the ghost of Banquo. Macbeth now knew that the descendants of Banquo were destined to reign after him in Scotland. From this moment, Macbeth's heart had turned evil and he only thought of how to execute all the power that he had as the King of Scotland. Meanwhile, the witches vanished leaving behind a ringing laughter that filled one's heart with dread.

No sooner had Macbeth returned from the witches' cave that he heard that Macduff, Thane of Fife, had fled to England. A messenger told him,

Glossary
Cauldron a large pot used to cook food over fire
Dread a great fear of something; being afraid

'My Lord, he has joined the army which Malcolm, the eldest son of the late king, had formed to displace Your Highness and place the right heir, Malcolm upon the throne.' Macbeth was filled with rage hearing this. At once, Macbeth issued orders to kill Macduff's wife and children and all those who were related to Macduff. This cruel order was carried out at once. In his anger and fear, Macbeth's noble heart had changed. He had now become a tyrant.

Glossary
Tyrant a king/ general or queen who has complete control of a country and he/she uses his powers in a cruel and unfair manner

This along with many other deeds put the nobility against Macbeth. Many nobles fled to join Malcolm and Macduff, who were approaching Scotland with a powerful army raised in England. Meanwhile, when Macduff met Malcolm, the later decided to test his loyalty to Scotland and to him. So, as they were sitting together, Malcolm said he too was ambitious and would like to exercise all the power that rested in a king's hand. He said that he had a violent temper and would go to any means to get what he wanted, even strip the nobles of his country if they came in his way.

Hearing this, however, Macduff who had just learnt about the murders of his family members grieves for his country which had fallen to terrible dark days. Macduff said that he sought Macbeth for mercilessly slaughtering his family and also to establish some order, if he can, to his country. Malcolm thus, knew that Macduff was a loyal scot and finally admitted that he too wanted to restore order to his country. Others, however, prayed that the army led by Malcolm succeeds and puts an end to Macbeth's tyrannical reign. Everybody hated Macbeth and slowly, everyone started suspecting

Glossary
Temper a state of becoming angry very easily

that it was Macbeth who had murdered King Duncan.

While rebellion was brewing against Macbeth, the queen, who had been the sole partner in Macbeth's wickedness, was haunted by terrible guilt and hallucinations. She had started sleepwalking. As she sleepwalked, she kept rubbing her hands as if she was washing them and said, 'There is still a spot there. Come out, damned spot! I still have the smell of blood on my hands.' It was some time later that her guilt over all the evil that she had done, led her to commit suicide. Macbeth was now left alone with nobody in whom he could confide his evil purposes.

Macbeth too wished for death but it was only the approaching Malcolm's army that roused his courage. He was determined to die 'with armour on his back'. Moreover, the witches' predictions and the words of the spirits too filled him with a false confidence. So, Macbeth had shut himself in his impregnable castle and waited for the approach of Malcolm's army. One day, a messenger, pale and fearful came to Macbeth. He said, 'My gracious

Glossary
Confide to tell your secrets to someone whom you trust
Impregnable an extremely strong building that cannot be entered into by force

lord, on my watch when I turned towards Birnam Wood, I thought I saw the forest move.'

'You lie,' cried Macbeth. 'If you are lying, I shall

hang you by the tree. But if you are speaking the truth; you can do the same to me.' Macbeth now had his doubts and his confidence was faltering.

Glossary
Faltering walking or speaking in an unsteady or weak manner; stumbling

He was not to fear till Birnam Wood would come to Dunsinane Hill to fight Macbeth and now the wood was moving. Then, he said, 'Make preparations for battle. I am weary of living and would rather like to die.'

Now, it is impossible to make a forest walk. However, Malcolm had asked his soldiers to cut branches from the trees of Birnam Wood and to hold them in front in order to conceal their true numbers. Thus, as the army marched, it seemed as if the wood was moving. It was thus the appearance that had shaken Macbeth for he knew that all the evil that he had done in the past will now be put to an end.

A severe battle took place in which Macbeth though poorly supported by his army, fought the army of Malcolm and Macduff. He fought with rage and valour until he saw Macduff. He remembered how the spirits had warned him to be beware of Macduff. Macduff too had seen him and he wanted his revenge. The next moment, a fierce contest began between Macbeth and Macduff.

Then, as Macbeth fought, he remembered the

Glossary
Weary becoming extremely tired after doing a lot of hard work
Rage uncontrolled anger

words of the spirit, how nobody born of woman could hurt him. Thus assured, and smiling confidently, Macbeth said, 'You are wasting your time by fighting me. I live a charmed life which

Glossary
Charmed words that are believed to have magical power; an amulet

cannot be ended by anyone born from a woman.'

'Then, forget your charm,' said Macduff, 'The evil spirit whom you served could tell you that I wasn't born from a woman. I was taken away from my mother's womb before she could give birth to me naturally.'

'Accursed be the tongue which told me so,' said Macbeth trembling, whose confidence had given way, 'I should never have believed those witches and spirits. They have tricked me. They raised my hope high only to destroy them so ruthlessly. I won't fight with you.'

'Then surrender,' said Macduff. 'We will make a spectacle of you and show men, with a painted board hung around your neck, on which it will be written, 'Come, see the tyrant.'

'I shall never surrender,' said Macbeth, whose courage returned with despair. 'I will not live to kiss the ground where young Malcolm will stand. I can't bear the curses of the people. Though Birnam Wood has come to Dunsinane, and you who aren't born from a woman oppose me, yet I

Glossary
Surrender to give oneself up; admit that one is defeated
Spectacle a public show often done on a large scale

will fight till the end.'

With these frantic words, Macbeth once more fought fiercely with Macduff. In the end, Macduff cut off Macbeth's head and presented it to Malcolm. His army had won the victory. In a few days time, Malcolm ascended the throne which had been wrongly taken from him amid the acclamations of the nobles and the people.

Glossary
Acclamation a loud applause; loud approval or welcome

Post-reading Activities

1. Name the characters who were travelling through the wasteland?
2. What was the prophecy made by the third witch about Macbeth?
3. What was Lady Macbeth's plan to kill King Duncan?
4. How did the sons of King Duncan react to their father's death?
5. Who was sitting on Macbeth's chair during the banquet? Why did he feel guilty?
6. The spirit had said that Macbeth needed to be careful of someone. Name that person.
7. What was the prophecy of the third spirit?
8. Whose family was murdered on Macbeth's command?
9. Who was the rightful heir to the throne of Scotland?
10. Why had Malcolm asked his troops to carry branches with them?
11. What did Lady Macbeth keep repeating while sleepwalking?
12. Write five adjectives to describe Macbeth.

About the Author

William Shakespeare was an English poet and playwright, universally acknowledged to be the greatest writer in English language. He is considered to be the world's pre-eminent dramatist also. He lived in the age of Queen Elizabeth I when England enjoyed a time of immense prosperity and stability. He is often called England's national poet and the 'Bard of Avon'.

It is indeed strange that though Shakespeare is recognized as one of literature's greatest influences, very little is actually known about him. Whatever we know about his life comes from the registrar records, court records, wills, marriage certificates and his tombstone.

Glossary

Playwright a person who composes plays

Early Life

William Shakespeare was born in Stratford-on-Avon, the son of John Shakespeare, a glove maker and dealer in wool. John was a prominent man in Stratford. William's mother was Mary Arden who was the youngest daughter in her family. She inherited much of her father's landowning and farming estate when he died. William was the third child of John and Mary Shakespeare.

Shakespeare probably attended Stratford Grammar School in his childhood. When he was 18, he married Anne Hathaway in 1582. At that time Anne was 26, and already three months pregnant. After sometime his daughter, Susanna, was born. It is generally thought that he must have been in Stratford when Hamnet and Judith, his other two children were born in 1585.

Between the years 1580s and 1592, what Shakespeare did is unknown because no records of his life and works exist of that period. This period of time is often referred to as the 'lost years'. It is possible that he spent this entire period in London after leaving Stratford to escape a charge of deer poaching. Some records say that he was employed at a playhouse 'in a very mean Rank' during this time. Researchers make assumptions that during these 'lost years', Shakespeare might have tended horses for theatergoers or worked as a sailor, a teacher or a coachman. Some think that he might have been a soldier, a law clerk, a theater page, or a moneylender. He could have held several of these jobs or he may have held none of them!

Glossary

Shakespeare may also have spent the time travelling to far off towns or even to foreign countries. His plays suggest that he visited Italy, for more than a dozen of them including *The Merchant of Venice, Romeo and Juliet, All's Well That Ends Well, Othello, Coriolanus, Julius Caesar, The Two Gentlemen of Verona, The Taming of the Shrew, Titus Andronicus, Much Ado About Nothing*, and *The Winter's Tale*, all have scenes set in Italy.

Career

How Shakespeare first started his career in the theatre no one knows for certain. Whether an acting troupe recruited Shakespeare in his hometown or he was forced on his own to travel to London to begin his career, is not clearly known. In the year 1592 came the first reference to Shakespeare in the world of theatre when Robert Greene an eminent writer of that time mentioned him in his writing. While in London, Shakespeare lived alone in rented accommodations while his wife and children remained in Stratford. Why his family did not move to London with him is unknown.

In 1592, when an epidemic of plague closed the theatres, the versatile Shakespeare wrote sonnets and other poetry until the theatres reopened in 1594. The same year, he joined a newly formed drama group called the 'Lord Chamberlain's Men', serving there as a writer and an actor.

Shakespeare produced most of his well-known works between 1589 and 1613. His early plays were mainly

Glossary
Versatile able to adapt to many different functions or activities

comedies and histories, the literary genre which he raised to the peak of artistic sophistication by the end of the 16th century. He then wrote mainly tragedies until about 1608, including *Hamlet*, *King Lear*, *Othello*, and *Macbeth*, all of which are considered to be the finest works in the English language. In the last years of his career, he wrote tragicomedies, also known as romances, and collaborated with other playwrights.

Shakespeare's works are the greatest representation of art from Elizabethan England. They encompass the economic, social, and educational aspects of life in a nice, neat package. No other art form, including painting, could provide so much information about life in Elizabethan England.

Theatre in Shakespeare's Times

During the age of Shakespeare, all plays which were written had to be approved by the government's censor. This is because plays at that time were considered morally or politically offensive and could be banned. It was considered so very offensive that many a time the playwright would be imprisoned too.

Shakespeare presented his plays at inns, courtyards, royal palaces, private residences, playhouses and the Globe Theatre built in 1599. The playhouses in Shakespeare's time were wooden structures with tiers of seating galleries in the shape of a horseshoe. They could seat two thousand to three thousand people who paid two or more pennies.

Glossary
Imprisoned kept in prison in a captive state

It is believed that at that time the theatre lovers who were wealthy could pay extra to sit on the stage! The main floor, which was surrounded by the galleries, had no roof and no seats. A person could stand and watch the play standing by paying a penny. This area was called a 'pit'. Up to one thousand people could stand and watch performances in this area under a hot sun or dark clouds.

The stage of the Globe theatre was four to six feet above ground level. There was no curtain that opened or closed at the beginning or at the end of the plays. A wall with two or three doors leading to the dressing rooms of the actors stood at the back of the stage. These rooms collectively were known as the 'tiring house'.

Males played all the characters, even that of women! Actors played gods, ghosts, demons, and other supernatural characters. They could pop up from the underworld through a trap door on the stage or descend down to Earth from heaven on a winch line from the ceiling. The sound of thunder was created off stage, by beating a sheet metal. To demonstrate that an actor had suffered a fencing wound, he simply had to slap his hand against a pouch beneath his shirt to release 'blood' showing his death.

Globe Theatre

Although Shakespeare's plays were performed at different venues during the playwright's career, the Globe Theatre in the Southwark district of London was the place at which his best known plays were first performed. The Globe was built during Shakespeare's early period in 1599 by one of his long-standing associates, Cuthbert Burbage.

The theater that Cuthbert Burbage built had a total capacity between 2,000 and 3,000 spectators. Due to the absence of electric lights, all performances at the Globe were conducted during the day (probably in the mid-afternoon spanning between 2 p.m. and 5 p.m.). As most of the stage of the Globe Theatre was open air and the apparatus for sound system were poor, the actors were compelled to shout their lines, stress their intonations, and engage themselves in exaggerated theatrical gestures. The plays which were staged at the Globe were completely devoid of background scenery although costumes and props were utilized. There was no proscenium arch, no curtains, and no stagehands than the actors themselves. Instead, changes of scenes were suggested in the speeches and narrative situations of the plays.

End of Globe Theatre

The original structure of the Globe Theatre existed until June 29, 1613, when its thatched roof was set on fire by a cannon fired during the performance of the play Henry VIII. The Globe burned to ashes and could not be saved. At this time, Shakespeare had almost retired and was at Stratford-on-Avon where he died three years later at the age of fifty-two. The Globe was reconstructed in the year 1614.

Glossary
Spectator a person who watches something—a show, a game, or any other event
Apparatus the equipment or machinery needed for a particular activity
Proscenium arch it is a kind of an arch which forms a framing on the opening between the stage and the auditorium in some theatres